THE RIGHT TO PRIVACY

INTERPRETING THE CONSTITUTION

BITSY KEMPER

ROSEN
PUBLISHING®

New York

Published in 2015 by The Rosen Publishing Group, Inc.
29 East 21st Street, New York, NY 10010

First Edition

Library of Congress Cataloging-in-Publication Data

Kemper, Bitsy, author.
The right to privacy: interpreting the constitution/Bitsy Kemper.
pages cm.—(Understanding the United States constitution)
Includes bibliographical references and index.
ISBN 978-1-4777-7506-6 (library bound)
1. Privacy, Right of—United States—Juvenile literature. I. Title.
KF1262.K46 2014
342.7308'58--dc23

2013041433

Manufactured in China

CONTENTS

Introduction...4

CHAPTER ONE
You Can't Just Barge in Here (Can You?)...8

CHAPTER TWO
Prying Eyes and Ears...21

CHAPTER THREE
Keep Your Mitts Off My Stuff...35

CHAPTER FOUR
That's Between Me, Me, and Me—and Maybe My Doctor...49

CHAPTER FIVE
If You're Looking for a Tort, the Federal Government Can't Help...61

CHAPTER SIX
Get Your Nose Out of My Garbage...72

CHAPTER SEVEN
A Future We Never Imagined...83

Glossary...93
For More Information...96
For Further Reading...100
Bibliography...102
Index...108

INTRODUCTION

The Constitution is one of the most influential documents in American history, shaping not only American law but also the American way of life.

Can a teacher go through your locker? Read your text messages? When someone asks your religion, do you have to tell him or her? Most people will answer no. They might even mention their rights, as Americans, to keep that information private.

But they'd technically be wrong.

When someone says, "It's my right," what they usually mean is, "It's my legal right." Legal rights can be proved in or enforced by the court system. Our cherished American legal rights are defined and protected by the U.S. Constitution, which went into effect in 1789. Ten changes and clarifications, called amendments, were added to it in 1791. Those ten amendments are commonly called the Bill of Rights. Since then, and as recently as 1995, a total of twenty-seven amendments have been added. No new law can violate the original Constitution and those amendments.

Some people look at the Constitution as what the government can do and the Bill of Rights as what the government may not do. Grouped together, the Constitution, the Bill of Rights, and all the amendments are crucial to how this country defines law and our rights as Americans.

Where in those documents can you find the right to privacy? Surprisingly, the right to privacy is not listed in the Constitution. The word "privacy" doesn't appear once in the Constitution or Bill of Rights. And yet, American courts have shaped, honored, debated, and protected our right to privacy for two hundred years. They've done that by looking at existing laws and court decisions to see how constitutional principles apply to each new case. It makes no difference how long ago a law was passed or a lawsuit was won. Legality is what matters, not how long ago a matter was decided.

Well over a hundred years ago, in 1890, two legal scholars wrote an article for the *Harvard Law Review* titled "The Right to Privacy." Authors Samuel D. Warren and Louis D. Brandeis declared that the harm done by a governmental invasion of privacy might not result in physical injury but could cause equally damaging spiritual and emotional harm. With that article, the two men have been credited with the first concept of an American legal right to privacy and the need to protect against an "invasion of privacy." Courts have used their wording and logic ever since.

In *Griswold v. Connecticut* (1965), a Supreme Court case about married couples' right to use birth control, Justice William O. Douglas said, "We deal with a right to privacy older than the Bill of Rights." However, his fellow judges on the case disagreed as to where that exact right could be found. Justice Douglas explained that we have implicit and defendable rights that don't have to be specifically mentioned within the Constitution. He said the Bill of Rights creates "zones of privacy" that are broad enough to protect parts of personal life. The *Griswold* case is called a landmark case because it brought a new, unique, and, maybe, surprising result that shaped future case outcomes.

That landmark case, as well as many others, will be cited and discussed in this resource to show how our "right to privacy" has evolved and been defined.

Courts now agree that the federal government has an obligation to defend our privacy rights, and they declare we are entitled to protection whenever we believe we have a "reasonable expectation of privacy." But what is a "reasonable expectation of privacy"? It's more complicated than one may think.

CHAPTER ONE

YOU CAN'T JUST BARGE IN HERE (CAN YOU?)

More than two hundred and fifty years ago, the need for a right to privacy started to swell. Under British rule, government officials could walk into anyone's house at any time and take anything they thought would prove someone disloyal to the king of England. Using a general search warrant called a writ of assistance, British officials could search any colonial home or ship for smuggled goods. They were looking for proof people weren't paying taxes, money that was supposed to go to the British government. Colonists were frustrated with the intrusions, but they were powerless to stop the invasions of privacy. The searches were legal under British law.

Why did eighteenth-century Americans have to obey British law? The United States didn't exist before 1776. Before the Declaration of Independence was signed, people were living in the land now called the U.S.A., but those 2.5

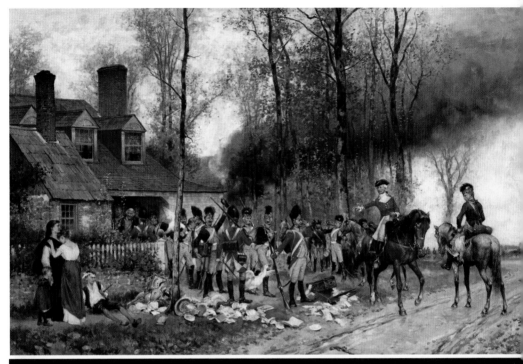

Intrusive home searches by the British military were common and legal in colonial times. The Fourth Amendment was written to outlaw this unwelcome and protested practice.

million colonists weren't Americans—yet. The original thirteen colonies were under British rule, and people followed the common practices brought over with the pilgrims on the *Mayflower*. No one had constitutional rights because the U.S. Constitution wasn't written yet. America hadn't been born.

Things began to change in 1761 when a man named Charles Paxton started to question the authority of the king. He went to court to plead the unfairness of the writs of assistance. He voiced his concern over the abuse of power the writs afforded. While he lost his case, it set into motion a rise in public dissent that eventually led to the Revolutionary War and perhaps even the Bill of Rights. In a way, the need for protected privacy was one of the reasons America was founded

Where does the law stand today? There's no single place to find the answer. While the phrase "right to privacy" doesn't exist in the Constitution, courts have determined time and again that Americans do in fact have such a right. The courts have agreed on and honored privacy rights that can be derived from the spirit of the amendments. In total, six different amendments have repeatedly gone to legal bat protecting the right to privacy, each taking on a different aspect of the issue. Each one is worth exploring in detail.

THE FIRST AMENDMENT

First Amendment (1791): *Congress shall make no law respecting an establishment of religion, or prohibiting the free exercise thereof; or abridging the freedom of speech, or of the press, or the right of the people to assemble, and to petition the government for a redress of grievances.*

The First Amendment protects citizens' privacy of belief. The wording of the first part of the First Amendment includes the establishment clause and free exercise clause. The two clauses make up what are called the religion clauses of the First Amendment. They state that the government cannot establish a national religion and that the government isn't allowed legally to prefer one religion to another. While the First Amendment secures the free exercise of religion, most privacy cases involving religion instead reference part of the Fourteenth Amendment, prohibiting discrimination on the basis of religion.

The First Amendment also guarantees freedom of the press. According to the First Amendment, the government can't control what is published, which means what the press prints might invade your personal privacy. However, media outlets can get in trouble if they publish false information, especially information that damages a person's reputation and harms the individual's business or career. Public figures, such as elected officials and famous people, defamed by the press usually have to show the work was written and published knowingly and with malice.

THE THIRD AMENDMENT

Third Amendment (1791): *No soldier shall, in time of peace be quartered in any house, without the consent of the owner, nor in time of war, but in a manner to be prescribed by law.*

This amendment protects the privacy of homeowners. It says soldiers cannot move into citizens' houses without their permission, even on government business. This amendment was written partly in response to the Edict of Nantes in 1685, when French soldiers were placed in homes with the sole purpose of harassing the families to stop practicing their minority religion. In addition, during the colonial era the practice of housing British troops in private homes was common. The colonists didn't take kindly to soldiers moving in unannounced and uninvited.

THE FOURTH AMENDMENT

Fourth Amendment (1791): *The right of the people to be secure in their persons, houses, papers, and effects, against unreasonable searches and seizures, shall not be violated, and no warrants shall issue, but upon probable cause, supported by oath or affirmation, and particularly describing the place to be searched, and the persons or things to be seized.*

This is perhaps the most frequently quoted amendment related to the right to privacy. Interestingly, if not frustratingly, this amendment outlaws "unreasonable searches and seizures" but doesn't expressly define what unreasonable searches

AO93(Rev.5/85)Search Warrant

UNITED STATES DISTRICT COURT
FOR THE DISTRICT OF COLUMBIA

In the Matter of the Search of
(Name, address or brief description of person or property to be searched)

**RAYBURN HOUSE OFFICE BUILDING
ROOM NUMBER 2113
WASHINGTON, DC 20515**

SEARCH WARRANT

CASE NUMBER: 06 - 2 3 1 M - 01.

TO: __TIMOTHY R. THIBAULT__ and any Authorized Officer of the United States

Affidavit(s) having been made before me by DETECTIVE, TIMOTHY R. THIBAULT who has reason to believe
that ☐ on the person or ☒ on the premises known as (name, description and or location)

Rayburn House Office Building, Room Number 2113, Washington, DC 20515.
See Schedule A

in the District of Columbia, there is now concealed a certain person or property, namely (describe the person or property)

See Schedules A, B, C and the affidavit submitted in support of the application for this warrant which are incorporated
herein by reference.

I am satisfied that the affidavits(s) and any recorded testimony establish probable cause to believe that the person or
property so described is now concealed on the person or premises above-described and establish grounds for the issuance
of this warrant.

YOU ARE HEREBY COMMANDED to search on or before _May 21, 2006_
(Date)

(not to exceed 10 days) the person or place named above for the person or property specified, serving this warrant and
making the search ☐ (in the daytime - 6:00 A.M. to 10:00 P.M.) ☒ (at any time in the day or night as I find reasonable
cause has been established) and if the person or property be found there to seize same, leaving a copy of this warrant and
receipt for the person or property taken, and prepare a written inventory of the person or property seized and promptly
return this warrant to the undersigned U.S. Judge/U.S. Magistrate Judge, as required by law. *The US Capitol
police are directed to provide immediate access to the property described herein.*

at Washington, D.C.

_____
Date and Time Issued
HOGAN, C. J. TH

Name and Title of Judicial Officer   Chief
Judge

_____
Signature of Judicial Officer
5-18-06
5:00 pm

and seizures are. In 1984, the case *Jane Does v. City of Chicago*, a class-action lawsuit filed by the American Civil Liberties Union (ACLU) on behalf of several women, helped clarify the matter. The courts determined that reasonableness involves balancing the need to search against the invasiveness of the search—the more intrusive the search, the greater the justification must be. For example, an officer cannot jail and strip-search a woman complaining about a parking ticket.

It's worth noting that if a police officer has reason to believe you are hiding something and asks to look in your house or locker or purse, and you agree, you have given the officer consent, or legal permission, to do so. He or she is no longer under obligation to get a search warrant, or an order from a court, to conduct the search. You have given up your constitutional rights to one. On the flip side, if you do not allow the officer access, he or she can still search once a warrant is obtained.

What if an officer finds evidence to use against you, but he or she found it through an illegal search or seizure? The evidence can't be used in court. In *Mapp v. Ohio*, a landmark case in 1961, the Supreme Court mandated that evidence improperly obtained should be excluded at trial. It gave the Fourth Amendment some new power and gave police departments across the country a strong incentive to do things the right way.

THE FIFTH AMENDMENT

Fifth Amendment (1791): *No person shall be...compelled in any criminal case to be a witness against himself, nor be deprived of life, liberty or property, without due process of law; nor shall private property be taken for public use, without just compensation.*

The Fifth Amendment protects privacy rights related to personal information and personal property. The amendment says a person doesn't have to reveal anything about himself or herself that might show or prove guilt in a criminal case. In addition, an individual's private property cannot be removed for the use of the government unless there is a legal reason and the removal is done in a legal manner, with compensation given to the property owner.

THE NINTH AMENDMENT

Ninth Amendment (1791): *The enumeration in the Constitution, of certain rights, shall not be construed to deny or disparage others retained by the people.*

This amendment helps answer the question, "Where does the Constitution say we have a right to

KIDS ARE PEOPLE, TOO (BUT WITH FEWER RIGHTS)

Everyone has the same level of protected privacy, right? Surprisingly, this is not true. Schoolchildren, in general, have fewer legally protected privacy rights than adults. Courts have recognized that youth live in a more open environment than adults.

They sit at group lunch tables, change in front of others in locker rooms, and spend the entire school day in an open classroom setting. Their world, by design, is less private. Since children are already living day-to-day with less privacy, the courts have reasoned that their rights regarding privacy should be less, too.

Some state laws specify that since school lockers are state property that students borrow, the state has the right to search lockers as

School officials are allowed to go through student backpacks and purses without consent and without a warrant, but only if there is a safety concern or reasonable suspicion of illegal activity.

needed. Lockers are different from, say, a student's bedroom. Schools own the lockers and give the students permission to use them, and as such there is no privacy given or implied in the use of a locker. Therefore, in some states lockers can be searched at any time.

Will they be? For the most part, the school needs a reason to search. The same goes for a student's backpack and purse: they can be searched at any time if there is a safety concern. Most attorneys counsel their young clients with a simple rule: if you don't want to get caught with something in your locker or purse in school, don't have it there in the first place.

privacy?" It means there are additional rights not detailed or listed in the Bill of Rights. It says that even if something is not mentioned specifically in the Constitution, it doesn't mean it isn't covered. In other words, citizens may still have a right even if the exact wording of that right isn't included in the Constitution or the amendments.

THE FOURTEENTH AMENDMENT

Fourteenth Amendment (1868): *Section I. All persons born or naturalized in the United States, and subject to the jurisdiction thereof, are citizens of the United States and the State wherein they reside. No State shall make or enforce any law which shall abridge the privileges or immunities of citizens of the United States; nor shall any State deprive any person of life, liberty, or property, without due process of law; nor deny to any person within its jurisdiction the equal protection of the laws.*

The Fourteenth Amendment extends the Bill of Rights, especially the right to due process of law, from the federal government to the states. The due process clause of the amendment states that people are entitled to a fair legal process before the state government can deprive them of life, liberty, or property.

Over time, the courts interpreted the guarantee of "liberty" in the clause to mean more than just one's right to physical freedom. The government had to be careful about limiting other kinds of liberty as well. States could not enact laws that restricted the freedoms of citizens unfairly or unnecessarily.

Therefore, the courts have interpreted the due

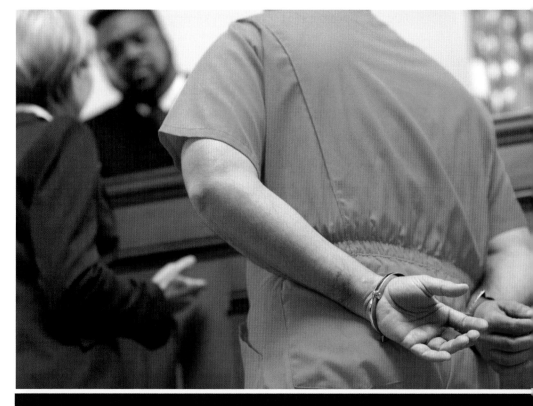

The Fourteenth Amendment ensures due process, which means regardless of the crime, all people are entitled to a fair legal procedure.

process clause to mean that not only must the state's legal procedures be fair, but the content of the law must itself be fair.

Many right-to-privacy cases are very personal. Right-to-privacy cases have called upon the Fourteenth Amendment to support a woman's right to make decisions about her own body, such as the choice to have or not to have a child, as well as in medical end-of-life scenarios.

Privacy cases are often controversial. They're also hard cases to win. Why? Regardless of the amendment cited, defining the meaning of a broad term like "reasonable expectation of privacy" is challenging. What's reasonable to one person may not be reasonable to another. Parents, for example, might have a very different view of what a reasonable expectation is than their teenagers. Who's right?

"Reasonable" isn't a standard that everyone can clearly define and agree on. It can be unique to every situation. A judge or jury has to understand the entire context of the situation before ruling on a case fairly: the people involved, where the events took place, what degree of harm was caused, which amendment was violated and how, and many other factors. They look to the Constitution and to previous court rulings to see how the law has been defined in the past, and if or how those definitions apply to the current case.

As technology and attitudes change, our laws change and adapt, too. But for over two hundred years, our Constitution has stood firmly as the backbone for every case brought to court.

CHAPTER TWO

PRYING EYES AND EARS

Our lives aren't as private as one might think. There are cameras at the ATM, inside and around banks and convenience shops, and sprinkled throughout department stores, apartment complexes, parking garages, and museums. There are red-light cameras to catch speeders or traffic violators, security guards searching purses and backpacks as guests enter amusement parks, and metal detectors at schools. All are preventive measures in the name of safety and crime prevention. But are they an invasion of privacy? Not everyone agrees.

LEGAL SEARCHING

People that view these kinds of intrusions as an invasion of privacy, and fight to stop them, usually file court cases under the Fourth Amendment, which requires that searches and seizures be reasonable, and that warrants for

Security cameras, even hidden ones, tend to be legal in public places as long as they aren't placed in a location where people have a "reasonable expectation of privacy."

searches and arrests be specific about the suspected crime.

When you agree to a purse search in order to enter a stadium, you willingly revoke your Fourth Amendment rights. But who is asking for permission to videotape you at the mall, street corner, or bicycle shop? The answer lies in the location. Those places are public. Others can see everything you do already, so courts have agreed the cameras cause no harm or intrusion.

In the mid-1960s, a man named Charles Katz was under suspicion of illegal gambling. The Federal Bureau of Investigation (FBI) tried many ways to catch him and decided to wiretap the public phone he had repeatedly been seen using. FBI agents recorded his calls, caught him in the act, and took him to court on gambling charges. The recordings were used to find him guilty.

Katz appealed the ruling, claiming that the tapping was an illegal search and that the use of the ill-gained tapes in court was a violation of his Fourth Amendment rights. The Court of Appeals agreed with the FBI. Since the wiretap was on the phone and not an intrusion into the phone booth, the court said it was legal. However, the case went to the Supreme Court, where the decision was reversed. *Katz v. United States* (1967) is considered a landmark case because it clarified a few things:

- It was decided that physical intrusion was not necessary to be considered a violation of a reasonable search, and wiretapping was therefore a search.

- Even though the pay phone was in a public location and used by the general public, the Supreme Court said that people making calls inside the closed-door booth had a "reasonable expectation of privacy."

- Conversations, even in public, may be protected by the Fourth Amendment if the conversation is held with a reasonable expectation of privacy.

Seemingly on the flip side, in *Smith v. Maryland* (1979), the Supreme Court ruled that a phone company could legally log calls placed by operators, since the caller is publically releasing the phone number to which he or she is asking to be connected. A public declaration negates the search violation.

EXPANDING THE MEANING OF "SEARCH"

The *Katz* case set the stage for other ways searches are, or are not, considered legal. With physical intrusions no longer the sole definition of a search, courts needed to clarify the exact definition of a search intrusion.

Several cases helped craft that definition. Fingerprints were declared usable as nonintrusive evidence in the 1914 *State v. Cerciello* case. Cases such as *Schwartz v. Texas* (1952) and *Cupp v. Murphy* (1973) helped decide that using a person's voice, handwriting, fingerprints, or physical appearance is not a search since these are repeatedly shown or left in public.

Fingernail scrapings and samples of blood, urine, and breath are considered searches as they are "bodily intrusions." As such, they require permission or a warrant. They are not an intrusion simply because they are uncomfortable but because they are, according to *Terry v. Ohio* (1968), a "severe, though brief, intrusion upon cherished personal security." A blood sample, for example, isn't considered an intrusion because a needle is required to get the blood. It's an intrusion because a blood test might show other private information, such as medication the defendant might be taking. Fingernails can still be scraped, and blood and urine can be tested, but law enforcement must have a warrant first.

In 2013, courts decreed that a DNA mouth swab is not an unreasonable search. *Maryland v. King* declared swabbing of the mouth for DNA samples to be no more intrusive than existing fingerprinting and photographing procedures. Now, anyone arrested with probable cause for a serious crime can have his or her mouth swabbed to see if the DNA matches evidence in the current FBI criminal database, regardless of whether law enforcement has a warrant. With more than eleven million samples on file in 2013, the national DNA

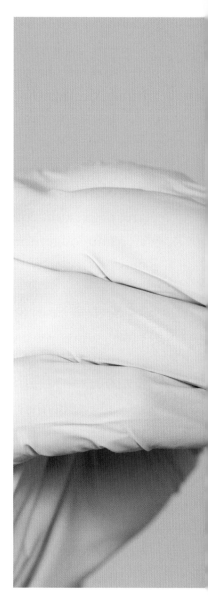

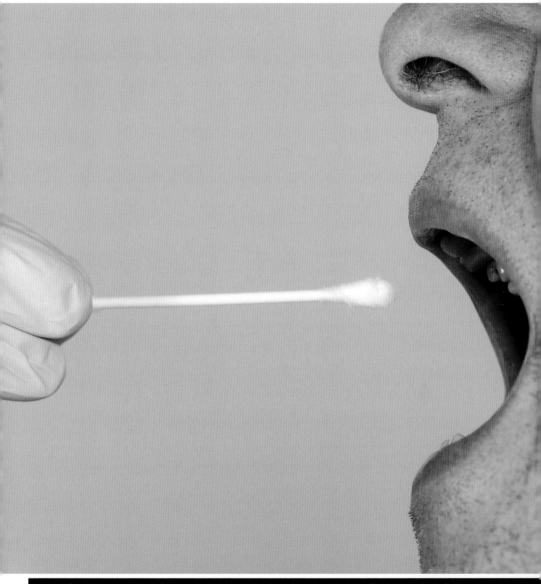

Those arrested for a serious crime may now need to say "ah." Courts have legalized DNA mouth swabbing, finding it to be no more intrusive than standard fingerprinting or photographing procedures.

database is expected to grow exponentially as a result of the ruling.

In May 2013, a man arrested for domestic violence had his DNA swabbed. It was found to match DNA collected more than a year earlier at the scene of an unsolved murder of a thirteen-year-old girl in Northern California. The man was arrested and charged with the crime, which had no other leads or suspects before the DNA match, according to the *Sacramento Bee*.

SPYING IS LEGAL, IN SOME CASES

Some experts have pointed out that today's level of digital monitoring feels like something out of a science fiction movie—and not an especially cheerful one. And the trend doesn't seem to be slowing down. Employee badges and security cameras at work can literally detail every minute of a person's day, even how long he or she spent in the bathroom. Companies say it prevents employees from "stealing time," not just pens, pencils, or computer equipment. But is it going too far?

Court decisions have upheld the right of employers to spy on their employees and guests. The U.S. Court of Appeals for the First Circuit has ruled employees in open areas have a "decreased expectation of privacy."

That makes it perfectly legal for employees to monitor open areas such as workplace lunchrooms and lobbies.

It doesn't allow them to be sneaky about it, though. The California Supreme Court stated that an employee who knows a conversation in an open office space will be overheard by coworkers can sue for invasion of privacy if that conversation is recorded by a hidden camera. Judges in *Sanders v. American Broadcasting Cos., Inc.* (California, 1999) rejected the notion of privacy as "all-or-nothing," stating there are some situations with an "expectation of limited privacy."

How private are public restrooms? For several years, Vic's Tavern in Hilton Head, South Carolina, was plagued with vandalism. People were stealing, breaking furnishings, and demolishing the men's restroom. In 2003, bar owner Charles S. Cole Jr. placed four cameras around the tavern to help put an end to the damage. One of those cameras was placed in the men's room. The cameras caught vandals in the act; the two men were so bold that they were recorded ripping the security cameras off the wall.

The vandals were later identified and arrested, all the while claiming they were the ones that were wronged. According to court documents, bar owner Cole stated the bathroom camera did not violate the

ARE CAMERAS INVASIVE OR ARE THEY HELPFUL PROTECTION?

Security cameras are there for the well-being of the community, to prevent crime. Footage may not tell the whole story, but it doesn't lie. Sometimes it helps convict; sometimes it helps prove innocence.

Valentine Garcia Sr. is a fan. In 2007, he was awarded $150,000 when surveillance cameras at a Greyhound bus station in Los Angeles helped convince the city council that police used excessive force against his son, who was shot to death by two police officers in 2004.

Juan Catalan is a fan of cameras, too, especially those of the *Curb Your Enthusiasm* TV show. He spent five months in jail for a crime that video footage would help prove he couldn't have committed. Catalan insisted he was at a Dodgers baseball game and therefore not near the scene of the crime when it happened. When his attorney scanned all the stadium security

04-15-2013 14:37:40

In 2013, officials zoomed in on security footage to help catch those who placed bombs near the finish line of the Boston Marathon.

footage, he came up empty-handed. When he heard a TV show was filming there that day, he scanned the show's crowd footage. There, in full color, was Catalan in the stands, chomping on a hot dog. Catalan was paid $320,000 in the police misconduct lawsuit.

Vancouver police pored over arena video footage after the Stanley Cup hockey riots in 2011, bringing charges against a possible record three hundred people.

In 2013, videos helped catch the suspects in the deadly Boston Marathon bombings. People from all over the world had no idea how critical their phone and home videos would become. Experts combed through hundreds of hours of professional and home video before zeroing in on the suspects.

When courts decide if security cameras are an invasion or protection, it's not always an easy answer.

plaintiffs' privacy because it "was in plain view, as evidenced by the fact that Mr. Suchocki stole it." Documents also show Cole clarified that the camera "was not in a position to record patrons actually using the facilities" but was placed to capture only illicit behavior. The Beaufort County Sheriff's Office incident report stated the bathroom camera showed the sink and urinal, where people could be seen from behind while using it, and the toilet could not be seen when the stall door was closed. An FBI agent advised the sheriff's office that the taping did not pose any criminal offense, and Cole won the vandalism case.

But it didn't end there: the bar owner was hit with a lawsuit from the vandals asking for $800,000 for invasion of their privacy and infliction of emotional distress. However, the case was dismissed, and no money was paid.

ISN'T THAT PERSONAL?

Most everyone knows it's illegal to open someone else's mail. But did you know the U.S. Postal Service has the legal right to record what's on the envelope, such as who sent it and where it is going?

Known as mail cover, this practice is a legal investigative technique. At the request of a law enforcement agency, it can be used to monitor the mail of someone suspected of criminal activity. According to the procedures manual of the U.S. Postal Inspection Service, mailing data can be used for several purposes, including protecting national security, locating a fugitive, and obtaining evidence of a crime. It does not involve the opening or reading of the mail (which would require a warrant), but only recording information on the outside of the envelope or package. Since envelope writing and

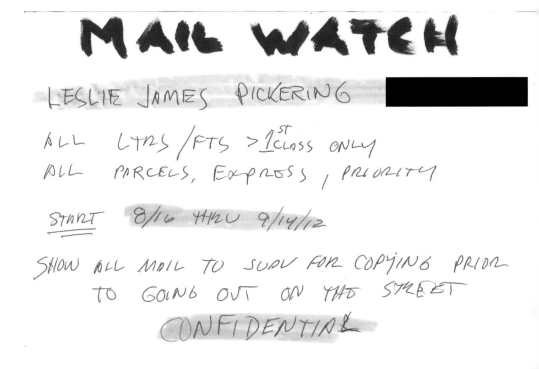

MAIL WATCH

LESLIE JAMES PICKERING ███████████

ALL LTRS/PTS > 1ˢᵗ CLASS ONLY

ALL PARCELS, EXPRESS, PRIORITY

START 8/16 THRU 9/14/12

SHOW ALL MAIL TO SUPV FOR COPYING PRIOR
TO GOING OUT ON THE STREET

CONFIDENTIAL

The U.S. Postal Service cannot open mail, but data from the envelope or package can be monitored and recorded. In this case, a man discovered a note suggesting his mail was being watched.

postmarks can be read by anyone who sees the letter or package, it's not considered a violation of the Fourth Amendment. Mail cover requests do not require the approval of a judge either. According to an article in the *New York Times*, mail covers are used to monitor tens of thousands of pieces of mail each year.

ARE BACKGROUND CHECKS LEGAL?

Many companies have background check procedures to make sure their hiring decisions are the right ones. The thinking is often that past performance and behavior is the best indicator of future performance. Typically, by applying for a job you are giving the employer the legal right to ask you questions about your experience and background and for the employer to perform a background check on you. Job hunters should know what employers can legally ask and check. They also need to know what information is considered legally private.

Laws such as Assembly Bill 25 in California prevent private and government employers from asking for social media usernames and passwords. Many "equal opportunity" antidiscrimination laws prohibit asking certain interview questions when the answers might lead to discrimination. The Civil Rights Act of 1964 is a federal law that says employers cannot ask about race, color, religion, sex, or national origin. Some states add items such as marital status, citizenship, criminal arrests, and military history. If anything uncomfortable comes up in an interview or workplace, it's important to know your legal rights. The U.S. Equal Employment Opportunity Commission (EEOC) is a good place to start.

CHAPTER THREE

KEEP YOUR MITTS OFF MY STUFF

Most women assume what's in their purse is their own business. Teens tend to think what's in their backpack is their own business. Most people assume what they do in their own home is their own business. But it's not that simple.

In 1761, fifteen years before the Declaration of Independence, a man named John Otis got fed up with the military barging into his house unannounced and uninvited. He went to court, stating, "A man's house is his castle; and whilst he is quiet he is as well guarded as a prince in his castle." He was asking for the court to recognize and honor the privacy expectation one has in his own home. He lost his case, but it started the ball rolling. Some historians think his case may have inspired parts of the Bill of Rights. At a minimum it confirmed the feeling that a lawful man should feel safe in his own home. The Third and Fourth Amendments secure that right.

OUTSIDE THE HOME

If something illegal is going on in your backyard or side yard, do police need a warrant to get there? It depends on how far outside the home it is. The law states that anything in the immediate outdoor surroundings of your home, referred to as "curtilage" in legalese, is protected under the Fourth Amendment as if it were inside the home. A front porch, for example, is considered part of the curtilage. Most open areas next to homes are considered outside the curtilage area and are fair game to be reviewed without a warrant. Interestingly, anything that can be seen in your yard by flying over your property, assuming the airspace can be accessed by the general public, is also fair game and not protected.

space can be accessed by the general public, is also fair game and not protected.

The area immediately surrounding the home, including the front porch, is protected under the Fourth Amendment. A warrant is needed to search it legally.

Let's say a man did something legal but unpopular. Can people picket loudly around his home or yard in protest? The Constitution guarantees free speech. In *Frisby v. Schultz* (Wisconsin, 1988), both sides agreed that public streets are open to all and that picketing is protected under the First Amendment. The court ultimately decided that residential privacy triumphs over public gatherings, though, and declared that homeowners have a reasonable expectation of privacy. The judge's final ruling in the case stated, "There is simply no right to force speech into the home of an unwilling listener."

INSIDE THE HOME

Personal belongings inside the home are legally private, requiring a warrant for search and seizure. But legal papers, bank records, and phone logs are not covered under personal belongings. Even if those documents were shredded and thrown in the trash, they would still be considered usable in court without a warrant.

Can your parents search your room without permission? Well, technically, it's not your room. It's the property of the homeowner. The homeowner is letting you use it. So, yes, legally they can search the room because it belongs to them.

What if you're an adult in the eyes of the law and living at home? Can your room be searched? In *Ward v. State* (Florida, 2012), an adult named Jasheene Ward lived with his mother in a home she owned. She gave police permission to search Ward's bedroom for drugs. The officers found a box that had drugs inside. Ward was charged. He argued his mother lacked the authority to consent to a search of his bedroom. The

A landlord can give permission to enter and search a house but does not have the authority to consent to a search of another person's belongings or personal items.

trial court disagreed and ruled in favor of the state. Ward appealed. The final ruling said that no one can validly consent to a search of someone else's personal property, unless the person giving consent actually uses or exercises control over that property. In this case, Ward's mother could legally consent to a search of a home that she owns and in which she resides. But she was not authorized to consent to a search of a box that did not belong to her and that she never interacted with. According to the court, police exceeded the scope of the mother's consent when the drugs were discovered, and the drugs should have been suppressed as evidence. The ruling was reversed.

IN AND AROUND SCHOOL

At school, officials are viewed as taking the place of parents with regard to making decisions in the best interest of the child. Attorneys use the term *in loco parentis*, a Latin phrase that means "in the place of a parent." Principals and teachers struggle with the balance of befriending students while gaining and maintaining trust and respect. It's sometimes hard to be convinced that school officials have

your best interests in mind, but they usually do. (If they wanted to mess with you, they'd probably pick a different career.)

Laws vary by state, but typically teachers and principals have the right to use drug-sniffing dogs without notice or permission if they reasonably suspect illegal activity in the school.

Some state laws indicate that a student's locker is school property, so the school can search it. But in other states, school officials must have "reasonable suspicion" that you are hiding something illegal before they can search your locker. Often a second adult is required to be present. Attorneys advise that the easiest way to stay out of trouble is to avoid keeping anything in the locker you wouldn't want other people to see.

Access to a student's permanent record is monitored by law. The Family Educational Rights and Privacy Act (FERPA) is a federal law protecting the privacy of student education records. It gives parents and students the right to view and, if needed, request corrections to school files. It restricts who else can access the files without consent.

Recently, some states have become more proactive in protecting private information about students and preventing the use of that information to discriminate. New York State, for example, amended its Dignity Act in 2013 to prohibit discrimination against students on school property or at a school function based on their actual or perceived race, color, weight, national origin, ethnic group, religion, religious practice, disability, sexual orientation, gender, or sex. Teachers attend special training to ensure proper handling of bullying or possible discrimination by other students or employees. It's not legal for school officials to ask a student his or her race, religion, etc., but they are obligated to protect a student if that private information is the cause of discrimination or bullying.

OLD ENOUGH

The "age of majority" refers to the time in a person's life when he or she is no longer considered a child in the eyes of the law. The official age varies by state. Most states (including Texas and Florida) consider that age to be eighteen. In other states, the age is nineteen (including Delaware, Alabama, and Nebraska) or twenty-one (Mississippi). Upon the age of majority, one can do things such as marry without parental consent or give consent to medical treatment. Reaching that age, though, does not give the former child all the rights and privileges afforded adults. A student must still abide by school laws regardless of age, which might diminish his or her official right to privacy.

SAFETY FIRST

Metal detectors are considered a legal Fourth Amendment search because they screen everyone entering the building and not only those associated with any specific criminal activity. They are permitted in schools in many states because the schools can demonstrate a need for preventive measures, and the courts have ruled that a metal detector is less of an invasion of privacy than frisks or other kinds of searches.

California, for example, allows metal detectors in its schools, but it says they must be used uniformly and not selectively on certain students. The Supreme Court has held that "sniff searches," in which trained drug-sniffing animals are used on lockers, in a common area of a school, are not considered a Fourth Amendment search.

Many schools have added video surveillance as a safety measure. The cameras cannot be placed where there is expected privacy, such as in the bathroom or locker room. Official school policies should reflect the use of recording equipment or other safety measures in effect. Most states agree cameras should be openly visible or have signage reflecting the school policy. To ward off passersby, officials can legally ask

Since metal detectors aren't considered as invasive as a frisk, most states allow their use on school campuses where general suspicion about weapons or drugs exists.

anyone on campus for ID; most school policies insist visitors, including parents, sign in and out when on school grounds.

In *New Jersey v. T.L.O.* (1985), a student was caught smoking in the girls' room and sent to the principal's office. She insisted she was not smoking. The principal asked her to open her purse, where a pack of cigarettes was found on top. Digging further, drug paraphernalia was found. She didn't think the principal had the right to search her bag, and the case ended up in the U.S. Supreme Court. It was eventually ruled that school officials, unlike police, may search students without a warrant when they have "reasonable grounds for suspecting that the search will turn up evidence that the student has violated...either the law or rules of the school."

School officials may not search you unless they have a good reason to believe that you in particular—not just "someone"—broke a law or a school rule. If a teacher thinks she saw you selling drugs to another student, she can legally ask you to empty your pockets or search your backpack. Catching you once doesn't mean she can search your backpack anytime she wants, though, only under reasonable suspicion. And suspecting some students have drugs doesn't give her the authority to search all students. The search must be conducted in a "reasonable" way, based on the student's age and what is being looked for. Strip-searching is illegal in many states, and where it is allowed, there has to be a solid reason to suspect a particular student of having committed a serious crime.

The *T.L.O.* case impacted many other school-related cases. For example, when two boys were found in a Los Angeles school bathroom without a pass, the dean thought they were acting suspiciously and asked them to empty their pockets to check for drugs. The court in *In re Bobby B.* (California, 1985) decided the search was reasonable as well as reasonably related in scope, because the boys did not have a pass and the pocket search was not intrusive.

In seeming contrast, a student known to be a bit of a troublemaker was hanging out near the school bleachers when he should have been in class. A teacher suspected him of making a drug deal and asked him to empty his pockets. Drugs were found. However, the ruling in *In re Appeal in Pima County Juvenile Action* (Arizona, 1987) stated the student was doing nothing to raise suspicion, and the search was therefore unwarranted. Judges decreed the search to be illegal and no charges were filed.

THE OPPOSITE OF ACTION

Niziol v. Pasco County District School Board (Florida, 2003) tells the tragic story of a boy who brought a loaded pistol to his high school. He was killed that afternoon when the gun accidentally discharged while taking it out of his bag to show another student in the school parking lot. The boy's parents sued the district, claiming school officials knew about the gun but failed to take action to avert a tragedy. They claimed school officials violated the Fourteenth Amendment's due process clause by failing to protect the minor. He did not have the right to have his backpack go unchecked. The family won the case.

CHAPTER FOUR

THAT'S BETWEEN ME, ME, AND ME—AND MAYBE MY DOCTOR

From the start of one's life to the end of it, personal medical history might be open for discussion or observation. There are ongoing debates about the right to create a child or not, the right to refuse medical treatment, the right not to disclose having a disease or having been tested for one, and even the right to die.

IN THE BEGINNING

Starting at conception, the courts have been invited to regulate. Courts have declared that procreation is one of the basic rights of humans. *Skinner v. Oklahoma* (1942) declared that the right to reproduce is fundamental to the very existence and survival of the human race and outlawed mandated sterilization for felons.

In 1965, *Griswold v. Connecticut* kicked off several Supreme Court cases legalizing contraception, allowing partners the right to privately

49

In 1965, Supreme Court Justice William O. Douglas insisted constitutional law protects individual privacy, even if those exact words aren't found in the Constitution or Bill of Rights.

make their own decisions on procreating. The *Griswold* case struck down a Connecticut state prohibition on the use of contraceptives by married couples. Over the years, the courts have agreed people should be free from government intrusion on a matter so personal and private as "the decision to bear or beget a child," as stated in *Eistenstadt v. Baird* (1972). The decision in this Supreme Court case gave single people the right to possess and use contraceptives as well.

Roe v. Wade, a landmark case in 1973, decided that the right to privacy is broad enough to allow a woman to decide about pregnancy termination. The Supreme Court argued that our right to privacy is not unlimited but includes personal rights "fundamental but not absolute" pertaining to marriage, procreation, contraception, family relationships, child rearing, education, and abortion. The decision states government cannot override a woman's decision about carrying a pregnancy to term. However, the state can regulate abortion procedures once the fetus becomes viable and capable of life outside the mother's womb, as long as the law contains an exception to save the life of the mother.

CHILDREN'S CHOICE

As children grow, their well-being is in the hands of the parent or legal guardian. If a child doesn't want to undergo a medical treatment, parents can typically override the child's choice and give consent on behalf of the child. Some states such as Texas have a clause that makes it illegal for a child to refuse medical care. States such as New York have dedicated laws dictating the care of minors in emergency situations. Public

Health Law § 2504, for example, says if an ambulance has been dispatched, a minor cannot refuse medical treatment. If a physician determines a minor's health or life is in danger and waiting to reach the parent for consent would increase the risk, medical treatment can be given even without the agreement of the parent or guardian. In less serious situations, the emergency technicians can wait for a parent to arrive

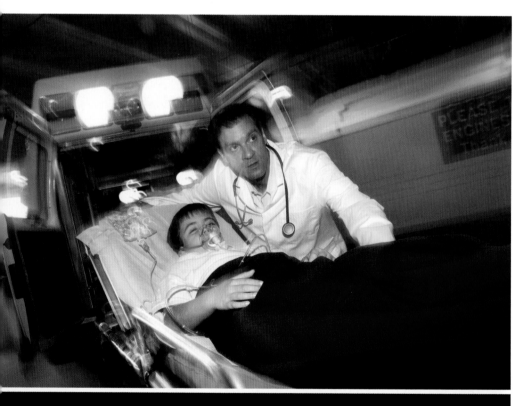

In emergency situations, medical treatment can be given to a minor without the consent of a parent or guardian.

before administering assistance or, if parents prefer, leaving the child unassisted. If there is serious threat to the child's well-being and the parent still refuses treatment, however, the emergency physician may take temporary protective custody based on state child abuse laws and get the child emergency medical help.

The illnesses a child may have, or the conditions he or she is being treated for, may be protected information. In schools, health files are kept private, but suspected illegal drug use can be proactively identified. Mandatory drug testing has been deemed legal in some circumstances, even though courts acknowledge it's an invasion of privacy. Whether school officials must have "reasonable suspicion" that a student is a user before they can make him or her take a test depends on where the school is located; laws vary by state. Random testing programs have been implemented in which officials test a few individuals or an entire class because they suspect "someone" is doing drugs.

In Oregon, a twelve-year-old student athlete argued it was unconstitutional that he was subjected to urine tests when he wasn't one of the ones on the team suspected of drug use. The Supreme Court decision in *Vernonia v. Acton* (1995) said that student athletes can legally be tested for drugs because athletic programs are voluntary, and student athletes are role models. Urine samples of all athletes on the team,

MY SKIN, MY CHOICE (RIGHT?)

Tattoos and body piercings are personal actions on one's body. Most people assume they can do whatever they want to their bodies and no one can stop them. It's their private body, after all. Minors, however, still answer to a higher power: their parents. Some states have made it illegal for youth under age eighteen to get tattooed or pierced without parental permission or a notarized document from a guardian. A few, such as Arizona, require a parent to be present during tattooing if the minor is seventeen or younger. At least twenty states prohibit or regulate tattooing of minors. A tattoo parlor may choose to set age restrictions for the business that are stricter than the law, as a precaution against lawsuits.

If you get a tattoo without parental permission, the tattoo artist violating the law could be charged with a misdemeanor and/or fined several thousand dollars. In some states, the tattoo parlor's license could be suspended or revoked. A parent may be able to legally force the child to get the tattoo removed. In many states, a child cannot refuse medical care. However, since tattoo removal is an elective (optional) and not a medically necessary procedure, not to mention painful and tedious, it might prove challenging to find a medical office that will perform the procedure on an unwilling minor.

regardless if they are under suspicion, are deemed constitutional.

TESTING AND DISCLOSURE

Some states require that minors have parental notification, not necessarily approval, before testing or treatment for disease. Schools and employers don't have the right to force anyone to be tested for contagious diseases like HIV. Both minors and adults have the right to refuse to take an AIDS test.

A person infected with AIDS or HIV isn't under obligation to tell anyone either, unless there is danger to others by not telling. In 1991, a Pennsylvania court overruled a request from a doctor not to tell his 447 patients and fellow hospital doctors about his HIV, including a patient that may have accidentally been exposed to his blood during a mishap in surgery. The doctor said informing patients and using his name in connection with the medical condition violated his right to privacy. The courts agreed that state law protected the confidentiality of AIDS test results, but in this case a "compelling need" overrode that protection. Since people were in potential danger, they deserved to know. Court documents from the case, *In re Milton S. Hershey Medical Center* (Pennsylvania, 1991), state: "The public's right to be informed in this sort of potential health catastrophe is compelling and far outweighs a practicing surgeon's right to keep information regarding his disease confidential."

Without a compelling need for disclosure, the privacy of one's medical test results is legally protected. In 1987, a neighbor's car ran into a woman's fence. At the scene, police cautioned the homeowner to wash her hands with disinfectant since the owner of the car had AIDS. Word quickly spread. The neighbors told

PROTECTING PEOPLE WITH DISABILITIES

When a person has an illness or disability, even if it's not something visually obvious, he or she can't be discriminated against because of it. The Americans with Disabilities Act, or ADA, was enacted in 1990 and amended in 2008. It protects a range of disabilities, including those that would only be known if disclosed. However, it does not force employment of a worker whose disability would create an "undue hardship" for the business. Employers can use medical entrance examinations for applicants after making the job offer only if all applicants (regardless of disability) must take it. Results must be treated as a confidential medical record.

other neighbors and classmates. Local television stations and newspapers got involved, and soon the infected man, his family, and their kids were ostracized. Nineteen children were removed from the school the man's children attended. In court, judges declared it was not an appropriate sharing of information, stating the disclosure was of no interest to society or government, and the man and his family had the right to privacy. By the time the ruling of *Doe v. Borough of Barrington* (New Jersey, 1990) came, it was three years later and the man had passed away.

DECISIONS, DECISIONS

Choosing whether to live or die is a personal matter. In *Gilgunn v. Massachusetts General Hospital* (Massachusetts, 1995), a daughter said her comatose mother would have chosen to live despite her irreversible neurological damage and would have wanted anything medically possible to help her stay alive. The hospital thought such care would be futile and issued a "do not resuscitate" order despite the daughter's request. When the woman died, her daughter took the case to court, claiming neglect. She lost. The daughter may have felt it wasn't right not to resuscitate, but it was legal.

Some terminally ill patients make it clear they aren't looking forward to drawn-out medical care

and go so far as to request a "physician-assisted suicide." This means a doctor helps them take a lethal
dose of a drug to hasten death. But this act is illegal.
In March 1995, the Ninth Circuit determined the
right to die is not protected by the Constitution, not
even under the right to privacy, except when it comes
to withdrawal of life-sustaining medical treatment. If
a person wants to refuse medical treatment, even if

Outside the Supreme Court a woman protests the federal
government's power to block doctors from helping terminally
ill patients end their own lives.

doing so would result in death, he or she has the legal right.

The Supreme Court determined in *Cruzan v. Director, Missouri Department of Health* (1990) that a competent person has a constitutionally protected liberty interest to refuse medical treatment. Knowingly prescribing or injecting life-ending medication into a patient is a different story. Most states explain it by clarifying the difference between letting patients die and making them.

Some parents are against medical intervention altogether. If parental decisions leave their children with inadequate medical care, courts must step in to decide between the parents' wishes and physician's concerns. Under the doctrine of *parens patriae*, the state's parental interest in children, a child's health cannot be seriously jeopardized because of the parent's choice. A parent does not have the authority to forbid saving the child's life. *Jacobson v. Massachusetts* (1905), for example, clarified the state's right to vaccinate a child against communicable disease even against a parent's religious objections. Although *Prince v. Massachusetts* (1944) was a child labor law case, it further set the stage for medical protection of a child. In the majority opinion, Justice Wiley Rutledge wrote, "The right to practice religion freely does not include the liberty to expose the community or child...to ill health or death."

Regardless of one's opinion on the matter, almost all personal medical information can be legally kept private. No one has the right to know what you are doing at the doctor's office, why you are there, or what may happen as a result of the visit. Schools and bosses can ask where you are going (the doctor's) but cannot ask why.

CHAPTER FIVE

IF YOU'RE LOOKING FOR A TORT, THE FEDERAL GOVERNMENT CAN'T HELP

The federal government can protect your house from search and seizure from an officer of the law, or against government action. But what happens when a colleague, salesclerk, or news reporter gets overly nosy? An invasion of privacy by friends or neighbors is a different courthouse altogether.

An action that causes harm to a fellow citizen but that is not a crime is called a tort. Torts are handled in a civil court. A tort is when you sue your neighbor for the damage created by his runaway lawnmower, for example. If your neighbor is found liable for the damage, the neighbor must compensate you with money.

A case involving the right to privacy against another person or the media is considered a tort. Invasion of privacy torts, like other torts, are generally controlled by state laws. In 1905, Georgia became the first state to establish the tort of invasion of privacy. Now, the vast majority of U.S. jurisdictions allow civil actions for this claim.

In 1960, the dean of the College of Law at the University of California at Berkeley wrote an article called "Privacy" that is still widely referenced today. In it, he detailed four different kinds of tort categories involving privacy: intrusion, public disclosure of private facts, false light, and appropriation. The outcome sought for each is the same: to be left alone.

INTRUSION UPON SECLUSION

According to the American Law Institute, in a tort case that involves "intrusion upon seclusion or solitude," the aggrieved party must prove the intrusion would be "highly offensive to a reasonable person." That's vague and open to interpretation; everyone, including court judges, has differing definitions of what is "highly offensive." Intrusion torts are far from black and white.

In these kinds of cases, the plaintiff does not have to show that any information or photography was made public in order to be considered a violation. In the case of *In re the Marriage of Jeffrey E. Tiggs and Cathy J. Tiggs* (Iowa 2008), a husband installed a video camera inside an alarm clock over the master bed, unbeknown to his wife. When she reviewed the tape, it contained nothing of a demeaning nature. She could not prove any damage was done to her reputation, nor could she prove her husband shared the results with anyone else. She nonetheless sued her husband for invasion of privacy and was awarded $22,500 in damages. She didn't need evidence that the video was publicized to prove her rights were violated. The Iowa Supreme Court said the wife "had a

As technology gets smaller, the risk of being recorded without one's knowledge grows. In an invasion tort case, a plaintiff can win without proving harm.

reasonable expectation that her activities in the bedroom of the home were private when she was alone in that room." The court also said that the "wrongfulness of the conduct springs not from the specific nature of the recorded activities, but instead from the fact that Cathy's activities were recorded without her knowledge and consent at a time and place and under circumstances in which she had a reasonable expectation of privacy." The fact that the tape was not shown to others did not affect the merits of her claim.

PUBLIC DISCLOSURE OF PRIVATE, EMBARRASSING FACTS

This tort is exactly as it sounds: publically displaying or distributing someone else's private information without his or her permission. This tort involves private, factual details being made public. Legal action may be taken under this category if someone publicly reveals truthful information about another person or party that is not of public concern and that a reasonable person would find offensive if made public. The level of fame of the person bears no weight. An invasion of privacy claim of this sort must be weighed against the First Amendment's protection of free speech.

If a woman went to get a large tattoo removed from a private area of her body and agreed to let the process be filmed for educational purposes only, but finds out the video was shown to the public in a movie theater, this is an invasion of her privacy. That woman's tattoo removal is not of public concern and the documentation of it would be embarrassing, if not offensive, to the woman.

However, publishing an article about a politician known for his family values but who is having an affair is of public concern and therefore is not considered an invasion of his privacy. It's a balance between the right to be left alone and the right of the public to know.

PLACING IN A FALSE LIGHT IN THE PUBLIC EYE

The false light defense requires the false information to be made public. It is not required that the information be derogatory, just objectionably false. A picture of an honest taxi driver in an article about cheating drivers, for example, is an invasion of privacy in that it places the honest cab driver in a false light. A photo of a person using a hula hoop published in an article on hula hoops is not considered an invasion of privacy, nor is a picture of a famous soccer player in an article on soccer, even if neither agreed to the use of his likeness. In the case *Beverley v. Choices*

SUE ME

A minor is protected against many things but not lawsuits or criminal convictions. Young people can sue and be sued, such as for damages to personal property, and they can be convicted of crimes.

A young woman appears before a judge in juvenile court.

Legal actions are split into two categories: civil and criminal. In a civil lawsuit, typically one party sues another for monetary damages for a wrong that was committed. Minors can advocate for their own legal rights in a civil case as long as they have a responsible adult (such as a parent) to protect the child and pursue the case in the child's name.

Criminal cases are between the state, acting on behalf of society, and the supposed lawbreaker. A child's age and experience impact a court's decision, but there is no official age at which a

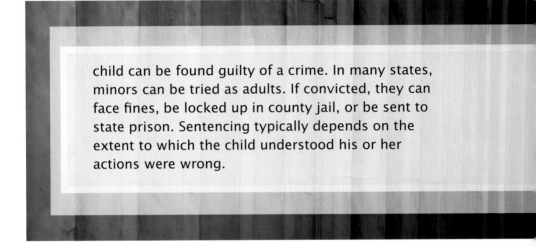

child can be found guilty of a crime. In many states, minors can be tried as adults. If convicted, they can face fines, be locked up in county jail, or be sent to state prison. Sentencing typically depends on the extent to which the child understood his or her actions were wrong.

Women's Medical Center, Inc. (New York, 1991), a doctor was awarded $75,700 for her unauthorized photo in a medical center's promotional calendar, as it encouraged a false assumption that she advocated the center.

There is a legal difference between placing someone in a false light and having some fun. The *Salek v. Passaic Collegiate School* (New Jersey, 1992) case was based on the "Funny Pages" portion of the school's yearbook. A teacher was upset over what she felt was an inappropriate caption under a photo of her and another teacher. She sued for defamation and false light. The law requires "proof of falsity," and in this case it was decided the image and caption were so obviously a parody and satire that no false image was created. She lost.

APPROPRIATION

This tort typically involves a famous person falsely being associated with something. It concerns someone using the name, picture, likeness, or persona of an unwilling or uninvolved person for his or her own purpose, usually for commercial gain or profit. The most common example is using someone's likeness in

Paris Hilton sued Hallmark for appropriation after it produced this card. Hilton had not given Hallmark permission to use her likeness or her trademarked catchphrase, "That's hot."

a commercial. While anyone may take a picture of a celebrity in a public place, that photo cannot be used for a direct commercial purpose without the person's permission. You couldn't paste it on a soup can, for example, to imply the celebrity was a fan of the soup company.

There are exceptions for newsworthy uses, such as using a person's photo in an article about a controversy on which that person has taken a stand. This category includes noncommercial usage, such as truthfully claiming that the person is a member of a particular advocacy group or has signed his or her name to a petition. Using a clip of a magician's act would be newsworthy and acceptable, but showing the entire act would be considered appropriation.

Using a recorded song in a commercial without permission is a violation, as is using a voice similar to a famous person's, when it is used to imply endorsement of a product. In *Midler v. Ford Motor Co.* (849 F.2d 460, 9th Cir. 1989) and *Waits v. Frito-Lay, Inc.* (978 F.2d 1093, 9th Cir. 1992) performers Bette Midler and Tom Waits declined to lend their distinctive voices to advertising jingles. The advertisers proceeded by finding sound-alike performers who could duplicate their sound and stylings. Both performers won; Midler was awarded $400,000, and Waits received $2,500,000.

PUBLICITY

The "right of publicity" is a new tort category, recognized by at least nineteen states. It's similar to appropriation and often includes some sort of trademark infringement. It differs in that it is more an issue of property rights than a tort right. While the right of publicity extends to everyone, not just the famous, these disputes usually involve celebrities because they possess the names and images that help advertisers sell.

The main distinction between appropriation and publicity torts is that many appropriation cases will not survive the death of the plaintiff. California, for example, enacted Section 990, the postmortem publicity law, which extended the right for a term of fifty years.

Like a trademark, the right of publicity is a sort of quality assurance. Owners of both trademark and publicity rights seek to prevent others from reaping unjust rewards by taking advantage of the celebrity's fame and image. In *Motown Record Corp. v. Hormel & Co.* (657 F. Supp. 1236 C.D. Gal. 1987), for example, trademark laws were used to protect the "persona" of the legendary music group the Supremes even though the group was no longer together.

In *Carson v. Here's Johnny Portable Toilets* (698 F.2d 831, 6th Cir. 1983), the well-known "Here's Johnny" introduction of Johnny Carson on *The Tonight Show* was used in an advertisement for port-a-potties. The company was found guilty because of the unequivocal association the public would make between the phrase and Johnny Carson.

Celebrities may feel that they are frequent victims of invasion of privacy. However, because the First Amendment allows and protects freedom of the press, the media cannot be forced to refrain from revealing newsworthy items about public figures. The question is: is everything about a celebrity newsworthy? In today's media environment, it can be difficult for celebrities to claim that certain parts of their lives are not newsworthy, especially since they have become public figures voluntarily. Public figures tend to have less success with public disclosure and false light claims and tend to be more successful recuperating losses from appropriation, publicity, and intrusion.

CHAPTER SIX

GET YOUR NOSE OUT OF MY GARBAGE

Television crime shows portray detectives following a suspect into a café and dusting the discarded coffee cup for fingerprints. As mentioned earlier, that is legal because fingerprints left in public places are public, and finding them is not an invasion of privacy. Trash is considered public property. Anything found in the garbage can be used as evidence in court.

Paparazzi or investigators can uncover all kinds of personal information from a trash bin. Garbage can tell of a person's comings and goings; finders can make assumptions about what the owners have been up to. In July 2013, police used DNA from a discarded water bottle to solve an almost fifty-year mystery surrounding Albert DeSalvo, a convicted criminal who claimed to be the Boston Strangler and died in 1973. The water bottle belonged to one of DeSalvo's nephews. The nephew's DNA was a close enough familial match to DNA collected

Trash is considered public property. Any evidence discarded in a garbage can or elsewhere can be used in court.

at a 1964 murder scene that a judge approved exhuming the suspect's body for further DNA testing. DeSalvo's DNA was definitively found to match the DNA left at the crime scene.

KEEPING LEGAL TABS

Taking photographs and going through trash aren't the only ways to keep tabs on people. Frequent shopper reward cards collect item-by-item data on every purchase made in a store, which may seem harmless. But buying patterns can tell a lot about a person. The *Los Angeles Times* reported in 2009 that a grocery shopper slipped on spilled yogurt in the store aisle and smashed his kneecap. The man claimed the store, Vons, looked up computer records of alcohol purchases he had made while using his club discount card and threatened to use the information against him at trial. Vons denied doing so. The case was thrown out of court.

Lesser-known people are increasingly shaping the law in areas of privacy and the press. Reality TV, social

Camera shy? You might want to stay inside. Photos taken in public places can be used anywhere, as long as they're not used to purposely misrepresent you.

media, and the Internet are giving ordinary Americans a taste of celebrity, and that newfound (if short-lived) fame comes at a cost. Viral videos are often home videos made famous unintentionally. If you happened to be in a mall when a home video was shot and that video went viral because you were caught in the background with your fly down, is that an invasion of privacy? What if it made local news? National news?

A camera crew was filming models posing nude on New York City streets for an adult HBO documentary. A bystander who saw the gathering crowd stopped to see what was happening. She ended up being filmed as part of the crowd. Her clear image appeared on the program introduction, both in the crowd and in a close-up. She had nothing to do with the unclothed models, or the show, and sued for invasion of privacy. She lost. The decision in *Gaeta v. Home Box Office* (New York 1996) said that she voluntarily joined a crowd gathered at a newsworthy event and that her embarrassment alone could not support an invasion claim.

NEWS REPORTS

A policeman in Oregon obtained a search warrant to check for narcotics and stolen property in a specific home. The local TV news station was invited to join the officer in the search. The home was filmed, as was the

The media is required to respect private property, but for information that constitutes news and involves the public's right to know, it may be granted leeway.

couple that lived there and their four young children. The footage aired that night. The couple sued the television station for invasion of privacy. The final verdict in *Magenis v. Fisher Broadcasting, Inc.* (Oregon, 1990) was that filming the family's home was not "highly offensive to a reasonable person," and the couple lost the case.

In contrast, crews from several TV stations in Rochester, New York, were filming a Humane Society raid. The investigator had a warrant to enter a woman's home and seize any animals that might be found in an unhealthy environment. The woman saw the cameras and repeatedly objected to the filming. The court in *Anderson v. WROC-TV* (New York, 1981) found that the cameramen were invasive and declared, "What must be remembered is the news people do not stand in any favored position," and they need to respect private property like everyone else. The woman won.

The First Amendment rights of the media make it challenging for anyone, whether an average Joe or a famous celebrity, to win a privacy case. That's why so few celebrities file or win lawsuits against magazines, newspapers, and Web sites.

The information shared doesn't have to be damaging in order for someone to want to sue. A newspaper ran facts and photos about the sale of a home, including the name of the buyers and the price paid. The new homeowner felt he had the right to keep that level of detail from others. The court in *Bisbee v. Conover* (New Jersey, 1982) ruled against him, stating the sale was not private information and the publishing of the details was not highly offensive.

FANS GONE WILD

Sports enthusiasts have been known to get aggressive to the point that teams have sought out the legal need for privacy. Many states have obliged. For example, California penal code §243.83 prevents the distraction of a player or interference in a professional sporting event. The law forbids throwing objects onto or across the field or court with intent to interfere with the play or distract the player, as well as entering the court or field during the event without permission. New York ADC law §10-162 says that it is illegal for any person other than a sports participant to "strike, slap, kick or otherwise subject to physical contact a sports participant during a major venue sporting event, or to attempt to do so."

Owners of the arena or facility are supposed to place warning notices, but failure to post a notice doesn't negate the infraction. Violators of California's "rowdy fan law" can be fined up to $250 per infraction. Disruptive New York fans can face up to a $1,000 fine as well as a potential year in jail.

PICTURE THIS

People can sue if someone intrudes into their private space in a highly offensive manner. This tort can apply to anyone, but it tends to apply most often to photographers taking pictures of celebrities. Courts have found that celebrities must be in a location where they have a "reasonable expectation of privacy" in order to sue. This excludes most public places.

It may even allow photographers on public property to take pictures of celebrities on private property, if something is viewable from the public area. Paparazzi are basically telling celebrities if they don't want photos taken through their window, they should pull their shades down. Fed up with intrusions on his vacation home, in 2013 music legend Steven Tyler introduced a new bill in the

Paparazzi line up to get a shot of Lindsay Lohan. The media cannot be forced to refrain from revealing newsworthy items. But is everything about a celebrity newsworthy?

state of Hawaii to keep the media from publishing photos taken of other people's private moments. The Steven Tyler Act was approved in the Hawaii Senate but stalled in the state's house of representatives. Many considered it too restrictive of the media.

Restricting the media too much can impact the ability of journalists to investigate wrongdoing. However, focusing so intensely on the personal ups and downs of the rich and famous runs the risk of crowding out more serious issues. Many believe we need to strike a better balance between the public interest and what interests the public.

A FUTURE WE NEVER IMAGINED

When Brandeis and Warren said mechanical devices were turning whisperings from the closet into proclamations from the housetops, they probably had no idea in 1890 how true that would be in the twenty-first century.

Photos sent via e-mail, text, and social media broadcast all kinds of information about oneself, and they can remain in cyberspace permanently. The Internet has made it much easier to be publicly scrutinized, or worse, victimized. Cell phones, shoes, and cars equipped with GPS can pinpoint someone's exact location with great accuracy.

On-demand digital movie services such as Netflix monitor what you watch. They track what movies have been viewed and suggest titles "you may also like" based on what you've already downloaded or reviewed. That reeks of intrusion to some subscribers. The services claim it's not an invasion since the data they gather isn't associated with names and isn't traceable to any specific person. The on-demand providers view it as a form of customized customer service, not an invasion of privacy.

Global satellite tracking offers strangers more information than perhaps was intended. Right now, with the click of a button, crafty burglars can check to see if plants are blocking potential entry windows on

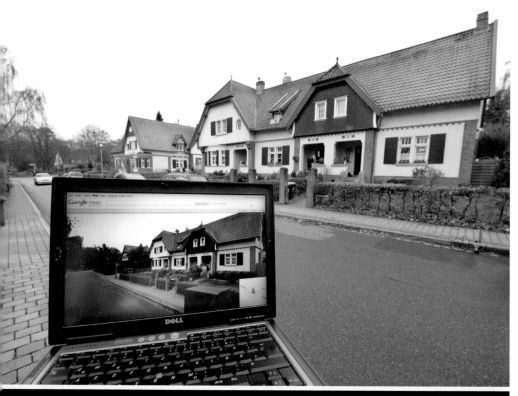

Modern, accurate mapping software has helped millions of people get from Point A to Point B, but some feel the level of detail provided is at the expense of privacy.

the first floor of your home. Mapping apps can be zoomed in to show your full yard, swing set, pool, and garden and give strangers a virtual blueprint. One's home is no longer one's castle but rather a public display potentially accessible worldwide.

IT'S JUST A TEXT

Social media brings new privacy concerns as well. With over a billion members, Facebook is practically a nation unto itself. Can others post or share whatever they want about you, without asking permission? In many cases, the answer is yes. Facebook offers privacy settings that help minimize invasion (for example, you can customize the settings so that you must approve a photo tag or check in at a location), but potential intrusions happen thousands of times a day.

In an interview with the author, high school principal Tony DeVille said that balancing the privacy of employees with students' right to free speech poses an ongoing challenge. "A student could post online that I have two heads and shower in the woods. Combine free speech with the fact I'm a public figure, not to mention that the absurdity of the statements make it mockery more than a factual reporting, and well, there's nothing I can do to stop them. It's not a violation of privacy."

GOVERNMENT INTERVENTION

As technology changes and evolves, so does regulation. The Privacy Act of 1974 was created to let people know how information about them is used and stored. It's a federal law that governs the collection, maintenance, use, and dissemination of personally identifiable information about individuals maintained by federal agencies, such as bank account and driver's license details. It prohibits the disclosure of that personal information without written consent.

The USA PATRIOT Act of 2001, in an effort to reduce terrorism, loosened restrictions on the gathering of intelligence, expanded regulation of financial transactions, and broadened the rules on immigrants suspected of terrorism-related acts. Federal agencies, for example, no longer need to contact you if they find it necessary to access your phone records, savings account information, or even library transactions. In May 2011, Congress granted the act a four-year extension, including its provisions for wiretaps, searches of business records, and surveillance.

The loosening of restrictions has been under fire, with some claiming the government has overstepped it bounds. Whether these legal provisions of the law are constitutional is what's under debate. In June

2013, contractor Edward Snowden leaked classified and confidential information about the workings of the National Security Agency (NSA). News reports based on the leaked documents revealed that while gathering data to prevent or counter terrorism, the NSA collected the communications records of millions of Americans. Many Americans, and even

Citizens protest the practices of the National Security Agency (NSA) in Washington, D.C. The agency drew fire after reports that it stores the phone and e-mail data of millions of Americans without their consent.

some members of Congress, expressed concern not just with the actions but also with their legality.

In August 2013, the Foreign Intelligence Surveillance Court declared the program constitutional and said it did not violate Americans' privacy rights. In the court's opinion, Judge Claire V. Eagan, a federal judge in the Northern District of Oklahoma, wrote, "Whether and to what extent the government seeks to continue the program...is a matter for the political branches to decide." That decision may be an ongoing debate as critics, such as the American Civil Liberties Union and the Electronic Privacy Information Center, continue to protest the program and challenge its legality. As of November 2013, however, the Supreme Court had declined to hear an NSA-challenging case.

STAYING SAFE ONLINE

The Children's Online Privacy Protection Act (COPPA) requires that Web sites and online services that are directed at children under age thirteen, or have knowledge that they are collecting personal information from children under thirteen, give notice to parents and get their consent before

A PERMANENT RECORD OF TEMPORARY ACTIONS

In 2013, several teenage girls sent a classmate, also a teen, some photos of themselves undressed and partially undressed. The boy uploaded the photos from his phone onto his public Twitter account. Since the photos were indecent and the girls were minors, the boy received a visit from the cops. Police served a search warrant and analyzed the boy's account, his computer, and his cell phone. The teen was arrested and booked into juvenile hall on suspicion of distributing obscene matter depicting a minor. The girls who sent the photos were cited for misdemeanor distribution of obscene matter. Even though the photos were of themselves, it was a crime because the photos were lewd and the girls were minors.

Many teens don't realize the long-term effects onetime behavior can have. Once something is on the Internet, it's often there for life, and it can be damaging to both the subject and poster. Colleges and companies routinely search applicants' social media accounts before admitting and hiring. Permanent records impact future employment, future relationships, and future self-worth. And they might lead to serious trouble with the law.

collecting, using, or disclosing that information. Revised in July 2013, the Federal Trade Commission (FTC) is restricting targeted advertising aimed at children and requiring that Web sites and mobile apps take extra care when handling children's cookies, geolocation information, photos, and other digital information. The changes also closed what the FTC called a loophole that allowed third-party plug-ins to collect children's information without parental consent. COPPA allows civil penalties of up to $16,000 per violation.

Identity theft has skyrocketed. Creative thieves repeatedly find ways to illegally access and use other people's money and financial history by stealing Social Security numbers, credit card numbers, and bank account information. The Fair and Accurate Credit Transactions Act of 2003 limits the publication of full credit card numbers on receipts and offers consumers annual free access to review their own credit reports. It also created a national fraud detection system and alert process. Consumers are encouraged to keep a vigilant eye on their own records to ensure their financial and personal privacy.

Having less privacy doesn't have to mean having less control. Fed up with frustrating telemarketing interruptions all day and night, Americans created the National Do Not Call Registry. The Economic Report

Biometric identification can simplify documentation by providing tamper-proof paperless ID, but does it create more privacy concerns than benefits?

of the President estimated in 2009 that almost 75 per-
cent of homes signed up for the blocking service. In
May 2013, the FTC proposed new telemarketing sales
rules restricting a payment method fraudulent tele-
marketers are known to use.

DO THE EYES HAVE IT?

A new technology used in India called biometric identification captures fingerprints, photographs, and the
unique makeup of one's eye through an iris scan. The
technology is used like paperless ID to prove one's identity and address without having to show legal documents
such as a birth certificate or driver's license. The national
program is supposed to empower India's 1.2 billion residents, especially poor and underprivileged residents, by
helping them with banking and government funding and
preventing abuse of government aid. Although voluntary,
the program is controversial.

Technology will continue to baffle and challenge
lawmakers, and society will continue to find ways to
redefine what is and isn't legal. What exactly is the
right to privacy? The answer isn't that simple, but the
fact remains: there *is* a right to privacy. A series of his-
torical examples and prior rulings have confirmed
Americans have the right to be left alone, even if the
Constitution doesn't use those exact words.

amendment A change or addition to a legal document such as the Constitution.

appropriation The taking of the name or likeness of another person for a commercial purpose. In tort law, it is considered a type of invasion of privacy claim.

Bill of Rights The first ten amendments to the federal Constitution, adopted in 1791, four years after the Constitution went into effect.

Constitution of the United States The basis for all U.S. Supreme Court decisions, this official document established the principles and laws by which the nation is governed. Adopted in 1787 and ratified by the states in 1788, the U.S. Constitution applies to every state, the District of Columbia, and all U.S. territories.

cookies Bits of data generated by Web sites and saved by a user's Web browser. Their purpose is to identify and store information about the user, such as login information for a Web site.

curtilage The land area immediately surrounding the outside of a home, including enclosed areas.

false light Intentional misrepresentation of another person that portrays that person in an inaccurate or misleading way. In tort law, it is a type of invasion of privacy claim.

federal Pertaining to the national government. Federal law applies to all states as well as the District of Columbia and all U.S. territories. A federal court has the power to review a law and strike it down as unconstitutional.

in loco parentis A legal doctrine under which an adult takes responsibility for a minor and makes decisions for him or her in place of a parent. The term comes from the Latin phrase meaning "in place of a parent."

intrusion Intentionally intruding, physically or otherwise, upon the solitude or seclusion of another person or that person's private affairs. In tort law, it is a type of invasion of privacy claim.

invasion of privacy The uninvited intrusion into the personal life of another, without just cause, which allows the person whose privacy has been invaded to bring a lawsuit for damages against the person or entity that intruded.

landmark case A standout case in which a new, unique, or surprising result emerges and is referenced in future cases.

legalese The formal language of lawyers that is often hard to understand; legal jargon.

paparazzi Freelance photographers who aggressively pursue celebrities to take pictures to sell to magazines and newspapers.

penal code A body of laws relating to crimes and offenses and their penalties.

plaintiff A person who brings a legal action.

public disclosure of private facts The public revelation of some aspect of a person's private life, without a legitimate public purpose. To take legal action on this claim, the disclosure must be highly objectionable to a reasonable person.

state law Law that is in effect within a particular state. State laws cannot undermine federal law but can assign more responsibilities to it.

Supreme Court The highest federal court in the United States, consisting of nine justices and having jurisdiction over all other courts in the nation.

tort A civil wrong resulting in injury or harm to someone else, recognized by law as grounds for a lawsuit. As a result of the lawsuit, the injured party may be able to recover damages (monetary compensation) from the party legally responsible for causing the injury.

warrant A document issued by a court that gives the police the power to do a search or seizure, or to make an arrest.

writ of assistance In American colonial history, a general search warrant allowing British officials to search any colonial home or business for smuggled goods, without specifying the location to be searched or the goods sought.

FOR MORE INFORMATION

American Civil Liberties Union (ACLU)
125 Broad Street, 18th Floor
New York, NY 10004
(212) 549-2500
Web site: http://www.aclu.org
The American Civil Liberties Union offers news,
    updates, and legal information and provides
    volunteer representation to defend and preserve
    individual constitutional rights and liberties.

Bill of Rights Institute
200 North Glebe Road, Suite 200
Arlington, VA 22203
(703) 894-1776
Web site: http://billofrightsinstitute.org
The Bill of Rights Institute educates young people
    about the words and ideas of America's founders,
    the liberties guaranteed in America's founding doc-
    uments, and how founding principles continue to
    affect and shape a free society.

Constitutional Rights Foundation (CRF)
601 South Kingsley Drive
Los Angeles, CA 90005
(213) 487-5590
Web site: http://www.crf-usa.org

The Constitutional Rights Foundation (CRF) seeks to
instill in youth a deeper understanding of citizenship through values expressed in the U.S.
Constitution and Bill of Rights and to educate
young people to become active and responsible
participants in society.

Federal Trade Commission (FTC)
CRC-240
600 Pennsylvania Avenue NW
Washington, DC 20580
(877) FTC-HELP [382-4357]
Web site: http://www.consumer.ftc.gov
The Federal Trade Commission is the United States'
consumer protection agency. It offers detailed
information on issues such as how to protect oneself from identity theft and how to control
personal information collected online.

Office of the Privacy Commissioner of Canada
112 Kent Street
Ottawa, ON K1A 1H3
Canada
(800) 282-1376
Web site: http://www.priv.gc.ca
The Office of the Privacy Commissioner of Canada
provides resources and information regarding the

privacy rights of Canadians. This includes investi-
gating complaints, pursuing court action,
conducting research on privacy issues, and generally promoting the public awareness and
understanding of privacy issues in Canada.

Privacy Rights Clearinghouse
3108 Fifth Avenue, Suite A
San Diego, CA 92103
(619) 298-3396
Web site: https://www.privacyrights.org
The Privacy Rights Clearinghouse is a nonprofit consumer education and advocacy project aimed at
raising awareness of how technology affects personal privacy. It provides practical tips on privacy
protection and empowers people to take action to
control their own personal information.

Reporters Committee for Freedom of the Press
1101 Wilson Boulevard, Suite 1100
Arlington, VA 22209
(703) 807-2100
Web site: http://www.rcfp.org
The Reporters Committee for Freedom of the Press
provides free legal advice, resources, support, and
advocacy to protect the First Amendment and freedom of information rights of journalists working

in areas where U.S. law applies, regardless of the medium in which their work appears.

U.S. Equal Employment Opportunity Commission (EEOC)
131 M Street NE
Washington, DC 20507
(800) 669-4000
Web site: http://www.eeoc.gov/youth/rights.html
The U.S. Equal Employment Opportunity Commission (EEOC) is responsible for enforcing federal laws that make it illegal to discriminate against a job applicant or an employee because of the person's race, color, religion, sex, national origin, age, disability, or genetic information. The Web site's Youth at Work section offers information relevant to the employment rights of youth.

WEB SITES

Due to the changing nature of Internet links, Rosen Publishing has developed an online list of Web sites related to the subject of this book. This site is updated regularly. Please use this link to access the list:

http://www.rosenlinks.com/UUSC/Priv

FOR FURTHER READING

Andrews, Lori B. *I Know Who You Are and I Saw What You Did: Social Networks and the Death of Privacy*. New York, NY: Free Press, 2011.

Bradbury, Ray. *Fahrenheit 451*. New York, NY: Ballantine Books, 1953.

Carper, Donald L., and John A. McKinsey. *Understanding the Law*. 6th ed. Mason, OH: Cengage Learning, 2012.

Carson, Brian. *Understanding Your Right to Freedom from Searches* (Personal Freedom & Civic Duty). New York, NY: Rosen Publishing, 2011.

Currie, Steven. *How Is the Internet Eroding Privacy Rights?* (In Controversy). San Diego, CA: ReferencePoint Press, 2014.

Eggers, Dave. *The Circle: A Novel*. New York, NY: Alfred A. Knopf, 2013.

Furgang, Kathy, and Frank Gatta. *Understanding Your Right to Privacy* (Personal Freedom & Civic Duty). New York, NY: Rosen Publishing, 2012.

Galiano, Dean. *The Fourth Amendment: Unreasonable Search and Seizure* (Amendments to the United States Constitution: The Bill of Rights). New York, NY: Rosen Central, 2011.

Judson, Karen. *The United States Constitution: Its History, Bill of Rights, and Amendments* (The Constitution and the United States Government). Berkeley Heights, NJ: Enslow, 2012.

Krensky, Stephen. *The Bill of Rights* (Documents of Democracy). Dundee, OR: Benchmark Books, 2011.

Kuhn, Betsy. *Prying Eyes: Privacy in the Twenty-First Century*. Minneapolis, MN: Twenty-First Century Books, 2008.

Marcovitz, Hal. *The Constitution and the Founding of a New Nation* (Understanding American History). San Diego, CA: Reference Point Press, 2013.

Merino, Noël. *Privacy* (Teen Rights and Freedoms). Detroit, MI: Greenhaven Press, 2012.

Orwell, George. *1984: A Novel*. 60th anniversary ed. New York, NY: Plume, 2010.

Porterfield, Jason. *The Third Amendment: The Right to Privacy in the Home* (Amendments to the United States Constitution: The Bill of Rights). New York, NY: Rosen Central, 2011.

Senker, Cath. *Privacy and Surveillance* (Ethical Debates). New York, NY: Rosen Central, 2012.

Sobel, Syl. *The U.S. Constitution and You*. 2nd ed. Hauppauge, NY: Barron's Educational Series, 2012.

Streissguth, Tom. *The Security Agencies of the United States: How the CIA, FBI, NSA, and Homeland Security Keep Us Safe* (The Constitution and the United States Government). Berkeley Heights, NJ: Enslow Publishers, 2012.

BIBLIOGRAPHY

Abrams, Douglas E., and Sarah H. Ramsey. *Children and the Law: Doctrine, Policy, and Practice.* 2nd ed. St. Paul, MN: West Group, 2003.

Alderman, Ellen, and Caroline Kennedy. *The Right to Privacy.* New York, NY: Alfred A. Knopf, 1995.

Amar, Akhil Reed. *America's Constitution: A Biography.* New York, NY: Random House, 2005.

The American Presidency Project. "Jimmy Carter: National Privacy Policy Message to the Congress on Proposals to Protect the Privacy of Individuals." April 2, 1979. Retrieved May 20, 2013 (http://www.presidency.ucsb.edu/ws/index.php?pid=32138&st=&st1=#axzz2hpVhg0Bo).

Antle, W. James, III. *Devouring Freedom: Can Big Government Ever Be Stopped?* Washington, DC: Regnery Publishing, 2013.

Beaufort County Fourteenth Judicial Circuit Public Index. "Pawey Suchocki, plaintiff, et al VS Charles Cole, defendant, et al 2006." Retrieved October 11, 2013 (http://publicindex.sccourts.org/Beaufort/PublicIndex/CaseDetails.aspx?County=07&CourtAgency=07002&Casenum=2003CP0701616&CaseType=V).

Beeman, Richard R. *The Penguin Guide to the United States Constitution.* New York, NY: Penguin Group, 2010.

Brandom, Russell. "Supreme Court Blocks Challenge to NSA Phone Tracking." TheVerge.com,

November 18, 2013. Retrieved December 2, 2013 (http://www.theverge.com/2013/11/18/5105360/ epic-nsa-phone-tracking-case-at-supreme-court).

Civil Rights Litigation Clearinghouse, University of Michigan Law School. "Jane Does v. City of Chicago." 1984. Retrieved October 9, 2013 (http:// www.clearinghouse.net/detail.php?id=9835).

Clark, Ross. *The Road to Big Brother: One Man's Struggle Against the Surveillance Society*. 1st American ed. New York, NY: Encounter Books, 2009.

Cramer, Maria. "DNA Links Albert DeSalvo to 1964 'Strangler' Slaying." *Boston Globe*, July 19, 2013. Retrieved July 21, 2013 (http://www. bostonglobe.com).

DeVille, Tony. Interview with the author. August 20, 2013.

Dolan, Edward F. *Your Privacy: Protecting It in a Nosy World*. New York, NY: Cobblehill Books, 1995.

Donovan, Kevin P., and Carly Nyst. "Privacy for the Other 5 Billion." Slate.com, May 17, 2013. Retrieved May 23, 2013 (http://www.slate.com).

Dowling-Sendor, Benjamin. "A Preventable Tragedy." *American School Board Journal*, July 2003. Retrieved May 22, 2013 (http://www.asbj.com).

Florida Department of Law Enforcement. "Parent's Consent to Search Adult Son's Bedroom."

Retrieved July 3, 2013 (http://www.fdle.state.fl.us/
Content/getdoc/691e1ed8-3902-4fbd-80c4-
b638f4d95ac9/12-03--Parent-s-Consent-to-Search-
Adult-Son-s-Bedr.aspx).

Fridell, Ron. *Privacy vs. Security: Your Rights in
Conflict* (Issues in Focus). Berkeley Heights, NJ:
Enslow Publishers, 2004.

Friendly, Fred W., and Martha J. H. Elliott. *The
Constitution, That Delicate Balance*. New York,
NY: Random House, 1984.

Gebert, Amy. "Cops Fear They'd Hire Bad Apples."
Sacramento Bee, June 9, 2013, p. A3.

Gelman, Robert B., and Stanton McCandlish.
*Protecting Yourself Online: The Definitive
Resource on Safety, Freedom, and Privacy in
Cyberspace*. New York, NY: HarperEdge, 1998.

Gralla, Preston. *The Complete Idiot's Guide to
Internet Privacy and Security*. Indianapolis, IN:
Pearson Education, 2002.

Haglund, Noah. "Suit: Camera Violates Privacy." *The
Island Packet*, September 10, 2003. Retrieved October
11, 2013 (http://www.lowcountrynewspapers.net/
archive/node/71263).

Kramer, Larry D. *The People Themselves: Popular
Constitutionalism and Judicial Review*. New York,
NY: Oxford University Press, 2004.

Kumar, Anita, and Lesley Clark. "Lawmakers Blast NSA on Privacy." *Sacramento Bee*, August 17, 2013, p. A9.

Kyvig, David E. *Explicit and Authentic Acts: Amending the U.S. Constitution, 1789-1995*. Lawrence, KS: University Press of Kansas, 1996.

Lesce, Tony. *They're Watching You! The Age of Surveillance*. Port Townsend, WA: Breakout Productions, 1998.

Long, Robert Emmet. *Rights to Privacy*. New York, NY: H. W. Wilson, 1997.

McGreevy, Patrick. "L.A. to Pay Man Cleared of Murder." *Los Angeles Times*, March 8, 2007. Retrieved May 1, 2013 (http://articles.latimes.com/2007/mar/08/local/me-alibi8).

Minugh, Kim. "DNA Match Brings Arrest in 2012 Slaying of Girl, 13." *Sacramento Bee*, August 9, 2013, p. L1-2.

Monk, Linda R. *The Words We Live By: Your Annotated Guide to the Constitution*. New York, NY: Hyperion, 2003.

Nazario, Thomas A. J. D. *Kids & the Law: An A-to-Z Guide for Parents*. San Francisco, CA: The State Bar of California, 2010.

Nixon, Ron. "U.S. Postal Service Logging All Mail for Law Enforcement." *New York Times*, July 3, 2013. Retrieved October 10, 2013 (http://www.

nytimes.com/2013/07/04/us/monitoring-of-snail-mail.html).

Rakove, Jack N. *The Annotated U.S. Constitution and Declaration of Independence.* Cambridge, MA: The Belknap Press of Harvard University Press, 2009.

Rakove, Jack N. *Original Meanings: Politics and Ideas in the Making of the Constitution.* 1st Vintage Books ed. New York, NY: Vintage Books, 1997.

Reporters Committee for Freedom of the Press. "Photographers' Guide to Privacy." 2007. Retrieved July 24, 2013 (http://www.rcfp.org/photographers-guide-privacy).

Savage, Charlie. "Extended Ruling by Secret Court Backs Collection of Phone Data." *New York Times*, September 17, 2013. Retrieved December 2, 2013 (http://www.nytimes.com/2013/09/18/us/opinion-by-secret-court-calls-collection-of-phone-data-legal.html?ref=charliesavage).

Scherer, Michael. "The Geeks Who Leak." *Time*, June 24, 2013, p. 22.

Schultz, E. J. "Bar Defends Use of Men's Room Camera." *The Island Packet*, October 18, 2003. Retrieved October 11, 2013 (http://www.lowcountrynewspapers.net/archive/node/71019).

Slauter, Eric Thomas. *The State as a Work of Art: The Cultural Origins of the Constitution.* Chicago, IL: University of Chicago Press, 2009.

Solove, Daniel J., Marc Rotenberg, and Paul M. Schwartz. *Privacy, Information, and Technology*. New York, NY: Aspen Publishers, 2006.

Standler, Ronald B. "Fundamental Rights Under Privacy in the USA." July 1, 2012. Retrieved July 19, 2013 (http://www.rbs2.com/priv2.pdf).

Supreme Court of the United States. "Maryland v. King." 2013. Retrieved June 5, 2013 (http://www.supremecourt.gov/opinions/12pdf/12-207_d18e.pdf).

Sykes, Charles J. *The End of Privacy*. New York, NY: St. Martin's Press, 1999.

Toobin, Jeffrey. "Annals of Law: Rights and Wrongs." *New Yorker*, May 27, 2013, p. 36.

Ventrell, Marvin, and Donald N. Duquette. *Child Welfare Law and Practice: Representing Children, Parents, and State Agencies in Abuse, Neglect, and Dependency Cases*. Denver, CO: Bradford Publishing Company, 2005.

Warren, Samuel D., and Louis D. Brandeis. "The Right to Privacy." *Harvard Law Review*, December 15, 1890. Retrieved May 1, 2013 (http://groups.csail.mit.edu/mac/classes/6.805/articles/privacy/Privacy_brand_warr2.html).

Zakaria, Fareed. *The Future of Freedom*. New York, NY: W. W. Norton & Company, 2003.

INDEX

A

abortion, 51
advertising, 69, 70, 71, 90
age of majority, 43
AIDS/HIV testing, 55–57
American Civil Liberties Union (ACLU), 14, 88
American Law Institute, 62
Americans with Disabilities Act (ADA), 56
Anderson v. WROC-TV, 78
appropriation, 62, 68–69, 70, 71
Assembly Bill 25, 34

B

background checks, 34
Beverley v. Choices Women's Medical Center, 65, 67
Bill of Rights, 5, 6, 10, 17, 18, 35
biometric identification, 92
Bisbee v. Conover, 78
blood tests, 25–26
Boston Marathon bombings, 31
Boston Strangler, 72
Brandeis, Louis D., 6, 83

C

Carson, Johnny, 71
Carson v. Here's Johnny Portable Toilets, 71
Catalan, Juan, 30–31

Children's Online Privacy Protection Act (COPPA), 88, 90
Civil Rights Act of 1964, 34
Cole, Charles S., Jr., 29, 31–32
contraceptives, 49–50, 51
criminal convictions and minors, 66–67
Cruzan v. Director, Missouri Department of Health, 59
Cupp v. Murphy, 25
Curb Your Enthusiasm, 30–31

D

DeSalvo, Albert, 72–73
DeVille, Tony, 85
digital monitoring, 28–32
Dignity Act, 42
DNA samples, 26–28, 72–73
Doe v. Borough of Barrington, 57
"do not resuscitate" orders, 57
Douglas, William O., 6
driver's licenses, 86, 92
drugs, 39, 40, 44, 46, 47, 53, 58, 76
drug testing, 53
due process, 15, 18–19, 48

E

Eagan, Claire V., 88
Edict of Nantes, 12
Eistenstadt v. Baird, 50–51
Electronic Privacy Information
    Center, 88
Equal Employment
    Opportunity Commission
    (EEOC), 34

F

Facebook, 85
Fair and Accurate Credit
    Transactions Act, 90
false light, 62, 65–67, 71
Family Educational Rights
    and Privacy Act
    (FERPA), 42
Federal Bureau of Investigation
    (FBI), 23, 24, 32
Federal Trade Commission
    (FTC), 90, 92
Fifth Amendment, 15
fingerprinting, 25, 26, 72, 92
First Amendment, 10–11, 38,
    64, 71, 78
Foreign Intelligence
    Surveillance Court, 88
Fourteenth Amendment, 11,
    18–20, 48
Fourth Amendment, 12–15,
    21, 23, 33, 35, 36, 44

free speech, right to, 38, 64, 85
Frisby v. Schultz, 38

G

Gaeta v. Home Box Office, 76
Garcia, Valentine, Sr., 30
*Gilgunn v. Massachusetts
    General Hospital*, 57
global satellite tracking, 83,
    84–85
Griswold v. Connecticut, 6,
    49–50
guns, 48

H

HBO, 76
Humane Society, 78

I

identity theft, 90
in loco parentis, 40
*In re Appeal in Pima County
    Juvenile Action*, 47
In re Bobby B., 47
*In re the Marriage of Jeffrey E.
    Tiggs and Cathy J. Tiggs*,
    62–64
*In re Milton S. Hershey
    Medical Center*, 55
intrusion upon seclusion,
    62–64, 71

J

Jacobson v. Massachusetts, 59

Jane Does v. City of Chicago, 14

K

Katz, Charles, 23–24
Katz v. United States, 24, 25

M

Magenis v. Fisher Broadcasting, Inc., 77–78
Mapp v. Ohio, 14
Maryland v. King, 26
metal detectors, 21, 44
Midler, Bette, 69
Midler v. Ford Motor Co., 69
minors and criminal convictions, 66–67
Motown Record Corp. v. Hormel & Co., 70

N

National Do Not Call Registry, 90, 92
National Security Agency (NSA), 87, 88
Netflix, 83
New Jersey v. T.L.O., 46, 47
Ninth Amendment, 15, 17

Niziol v. Pasco County District School Board, 48

O

on-demand services, 83–84
Otis, John, 35

P

paparazzi, 72, 80
parens patriae doctrine, 59
Paxton, Charles, 9–10
physician-assisted suicide, 58
Prince v. Massachusetts, 59
privacy, right to,
celebrities, 69, 71, 70, 78, 80–82
future of, 83–92
history of, 8–20
in the home, 35–40, 76–78,
medical scenarios, 20, 49–60
overview of, 4–7
in public, 21–34, 72–76, 79
in schools, 16–17, 40–48
social media, 74, 76, 83, 85, 89
torts, 61–71
Privacy Act of 1974, 86
public disclosure of private facts, 62, 64–65
publicity, right of, 70–71

R

reality TV, 74
rewards cards, 74
right to die, 49, 57–60
Roe v. Wade, 51
"rowdy fan laws," 79
Rutledge, Wiley, 59

S

Salek v. Passaic Collegiate School, 67
Sanders v. American Broadcasting Cos., Inc., 29
Schwartz v. Texas, 25
search and seizure, 21–28, 36–42, 46–47, 61, 89
Skinner v. Oklahoma, 49
Smith v. Maryland, 24–25
"sniff searches," 44
Snowden, Edward, 87
Stanley Cup hockey riots, 31
State v. Cerciello, 25
sterilization, 49
Steven Tyler Act, 82
strip-searching, 47
Supremes, the, 70

T

tattoos and piercings, 54, 65
Terry v. Ohio, 25

Third Amendment, 11–12, 35
Tonight Show, The, 71
Twitter, 89
Tyler, Steven, 80, 82

U

urine tests, 25, 26, 53, 55
USA PATRIOT Act, 86
U.S. Postal Service, 32–33

V

vaccinations, 59
Veronica v. Acton, 53, 55
video surveillance, 23, 28, 29–32, 44, 62–64
viral videos, 76
Vons, 74

W

Waits, Tom, 69
Waits v. Frito-Lay, Inc., 69
Ward, Jasheene, 39
Ward v. State, 39–40
warrants, 8, 12, 14, 21, 25, 26, 32, 36, 38, 46, 76, 78, 89
Warren, Samuel D., 6, 83
wiretapping, 23, 24, 86
writ of assistance, 8, 9, 10

ABOUT THE AUTHOR

As a nationally syndicated columnist, Bitsy Kemper has appeared on CNN and *CBS This Morning*. Her work has been in hundreds of newspapers and on radio and TV stations across the United States. Author of seven children's books so far, she enjoys a good laugh, spending quality time with her husband and three kids, and presenting at author visits and conferences from California to New York. Kemper is trying to find the fine balance between actively interacting online and keeping people out of her business. Find out what she shares publicly at http://www.BitsyKemper.com.

PHOTO CREDITS